{ CITIESCAPE }

BEIJING*

{ CITIESCAPE }

KORINA MILLER

CONTENTS*

VITAL STATS*

NAME Beijing **AKA** Yanjing, from the State
of Yan which existed long ago; Peking by nostalgic
Westerners **DATE OF BIRTH** 13th century as
a capital city; named Beijing in AD 1403
HEIGHT 43.5m **SIZE** 16,800 sq km
(Beijing municipality) **ADDRESS** People's
Republic of China **POPULATION** 14.9 million

PEOPLE*

{ * **ABOUT 97% OF BEIJINGERS ARE HAN CHINESE; THE OTHER 3% IS MADE UP OF A SCATTERING OF CHINA'S 56 OFFICIAL ETHNIC MINORITIES** – mainly Hui, }

Manchu and Mongol. The Hui are one of the most established minority groups, forming 2% of that remaining 3%. Distinguished by their white caps, they are often street vendors, dishing up roasted nuts and scrumptious nougat. Most Beijingers speak Mandarin, China's official dialect. The expat community includes Russian, South Korean, British and Canadian people.

THE ONE-CHILD policy has had an unsurprisingly huge impact on family life in Beijing. Beyond the obvious disappearance of uncles and aunts, each young couple is financially responsible for two sets of parents and grandparents. Their children are notoriously spoiled and referred to as 'little emperors'. Recent decades have seen the standard of living rise dramatically, but China has one of the world's worst divides between rich and poor and many rural families make their way into Beijing with hopes of eking out a better living.

9.

ANATOMY*

*BEIJING'S FLAT SYMMETRY LIES ON AN ANCIENT NORTH–SOUTH AXIS, WITH TIANANMEN SQUARE** smack in the middle and the Forbidden City directly to its north. At its southern end lies the Temple of Heaven, and to the north is Ditan Park.

MANY OF BEIJING'S ancient gates and buildings still stand, surrounded by the concrete blocks of the austere communist era, plenty of flashy modern architecture and countless building cranes. The city's boulevards, vast national highways and ring roads are crammed with careening taxis and buses, plus lanes so thick with bicycles that they move as one giant mass of steel.

BENEATH THE FOUNDATIONS of the Forbidden City lies Beijing's subway, which stretched a mere 38 kilometres when it was opened in 1969. Today's 110 kilometres of track is planned to become a whopping 1000 kilometres by 2050. Up above, flights from as far afield as Zimbabwe come in to land at Asia's busiest airport.

PERSONALITY *

{ ***EVER SINCE MARCO POLO RETURNED HOME FROM CHINA WITH TALES OF SILKY SPLENDOUR AND FANCIFUL INVENTIONS,** Beijing has captured the imagination of the Western world. Images of forbidden palaces, emperors, exotic food and teeming markets inspired intrepid explorers and romantics alike. Beijing's intrigue and mystery, and its propensity for delivering the unexpected, are mainly a result of its fascinating, turbulent history. }

IT'S A HISTORY that stretches back unfathomable spans of time. Peking Man, believed to be among the first humans on earth, dwelled here some 500,000 years ago. Settled as a frontier trading town for Mongols, Koreans and minority ethnic tribes, Beijing's strategic location on the edge of the North China Plain soon had conquerors quarrelling over it. In AD 1215, Genghis Khan descended on the city. His grandson, Kublai, made Beijing the capital of his empire (1215–1368), as did the Chinese Ming (1368–1644) and Manchu Qing (1644–1911) dynasties that followed.

13.

DURING THE FINAL dynastic years, war and rebellions took their toll on the capital, as did the Qing's brutal and incompetent rule. Left in the hands of two-year-old emperor Puyi, the leadership quickly collapsed, leaving the city near shambles.

IN 1911 the Kuomintang jumped to power and declared the Republic of China, but poverty and splintered rule soon led to more rebellion. Beijing's university bubbled with dissent and Karl Marx's *The Communist Manifesto* found its way into the hands of the library assistant, Mao Zedong (1893–1976). The communists soon emerged and, after an uneasy union with the Kuomintang that left many of them slaughtered, fled to the countryside to launch a civil war.

IN THE MIDST of all this, in 1937 Japan invaded Beijing and got comfy until the end of World War II. By that time the Chinese Civil War was in full swing and the communists, under the leadership of Mao, celebrated victory in 1949. As the Kuomintang fled to Taiwan, the communists marched into Beijing and proclaimed the People's Republic of China. This heralded a period of catastrophic upheaval. Beijing's huge city walls were pulled down, hundreds of temples and monuments were destroyed and buildings flattened. Beijing has deep scars from this manic and hugely violent mayhem.

IN 1979 China's new pragmatic leader, Deng Xiaoping, unlocked China's doors to the West. Temples and monuments were restored; glittering towers and high-rises erupted. While the government continues to control, coerce and censor, Beijing is now riding two very different currents – communism and capitalism.

THE CITY'S roller-coaster ride from the past into the future has resulted in an absorbing, vibrant culture, luring many to follow in Marco Polo's footsteps. The chapters that follow attempt to piece together the puzzle of Beijing – traditional yet bold, grand yet still ambitious, and always full of life.

14.

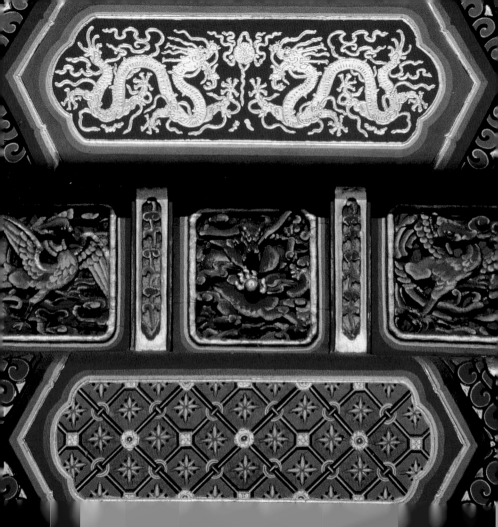

GRAND*

{ }

*PERUSE ITS HISTORY, GAZE AT ITS SIGHTS, FEEL SMALL UNDER ITS AUTHORITY – FROM ANY ANGLE, BEIJING IS GRAND.** With a magnetic pull and an influence that stretches over the country, it's at once humbling and awesome. Its beginnings may have been modest (it was only crowned capital in the 13th century), but you'd never guess.

KUBLAI KHAN ONCE sat on Beijing's throne, ruling over the largest empire the world has yet known. The city has also been called home by earlier conquerors such as the formidable Mongols, and the later successions of Ming and Qing emperors, as well as the 20th century's omnipresent Mao Zedong. Each helped to transform it into a cultural and political force that would determine China's destiny, and in their wake left jaw-dropping buildings, gates, parks and palaces to express their power and magnificence. Today these are still the enormous building blocks around which the rest of the city is built, giving Beijing its look of dignity and opulence.

17.

BEIJING IS ALSO grand in physical size, its immense bulk stretching out across 16,800 square kilometres – making it roughly the same size as Belgium. Its narrow alleyways and sprawling markets raise havoc with map-makers but are confined between amazingly orderly avenues, freeways and ring roads.

THE CAPITAL'S imposing voice rumbles throughout the country, having the supreme and final word on virtually everything. Within China, Beijing is the unquestionable king of the castle: whatever rolls up from Beijing must be heeded.

VISITORS FROM other parts of China are awed by the splendour they find when first stepping off a bus in the city; while there's definitely much to be awed by, their reaction is at least in part due to Beijing's prestigious reputation. It's one thing to see the city on TV; it's quite another to feel its immensity around you. And as if its billion-plus subjects weren't enough, the city's voice is also increasingly catching air waves around the globe.

BEIJINGERS THEMSELVES are more than aware of the city's significance. They walk with heads held high and are quick to fill visitors in on the brilliance of Beijing – proud of their city, but not arrogant. After the cultural austerity of the early years of communism, they have thrown off their navy-blue Mao suits, rebuilt their temples, got out their paintbrushes and restrung their musical instruments. As the government loosens its reins, activities once considered too bourgeois – from lingering in teahouses to burning incense at temples – are back in full swing. With both the contemporary and traditional arts blossoming again in the Middle Kingdom, it feels like Beijingers are making up for lost time.

SONS OF HEAVEN*

{ * **UNTIL 1949, THE FORBIDDEN CITY DREW AN IMPENETRABLE LINE BETWEEN THE GENERAL POPULATION AND THE WORLD OF EMPERORS,** eunuchs, ceremony and splendour. Twenty-four successive Ming and Qing emperors resided in it, many becoming absorbed in the luxury of palace life to the serious detriment of their rule and the living conditions outside the palace walls. Some wrote poetry rather than govern, while others collected huge harems of imperial concubines (Emperor Jiajiang had over 1000). Emperors were also kept busy tucking into over 100 different dishes twice daily, prepared by an army of 450 kitchen workers. }

THE PALACE WAS built by a million labourers between 1406 and 1420. It contains 9999.5 rooms, making it half a room smaller than the Jade Emperor's Heavenly Palace – a 'humble' gesture by the mere mortal emperors. Covering 720,000 square metres, a full-time restoration squad continuously repaints and repairs its 800 buildings; it's estimated to take ten years to complete a full renovation.

21.

THE ROYAL ENTOURAGE wanted to escape the excessive heat of Beijing's summer, but didn't want to go anywhere less grand than their downtown Forbidden City. The result was the creation of the Summer Palace, built in the hills of Beijing's outskirts inside enormous grounds dotted with temples, gardens, pavilions and corridors. To give an idea of the excesses of the dynastic leaders, it contains a huge marble boat built by Empress Dowager Cixi in 1878 with money earmarked for a modern navy.

THE GREAT WALL *

{ *** STRETCHING MORE THAN 5000 KILOMETRES, IT'S DIFFICULT TO FATHOM THE ENORMITY OF THE GREAT WALL.** It's only as you peer from one of its lookouts and see it snaking its way through the mountains that you begin to get an inkling. }

THE WALL WAS initially built by the tyrannical Emperor Qin (221–206 BC), who indentured thousands of labourers to link existing city walls in hopes of keeping out the Mongols. Over the centuries, the wall crumbled and was rebuilt numerous times; its vastness required huge quantities of maintenance and countless people to man it. In the end the Mongols swept over and through the wall anyway, and established a capital in present-day Beijing within the wall's shade.

NEVERTHELESS, THE WALL has served many a mighty purpose. It was a means of unifying China (what better way to create 'us and them'?); an excellent transport thoroughfare; an important link on the Silk Road; and now receives an estimated 10 million visitors annually.

24.

TIANANMEN SQUARE *

{ * **CONCEIVED BY MAO TO DEMONSTRATE THE MIGHT OF THE COMMUNIST PARTY, TIANANMEN SQUARE IS A CONCRETE DESERT OF PAVING STONES...** until kites fill the sky above it, children stamp around on it and tourists snap photos of it, the world's largest public square. Mao reviewed parades of up to a million young Red Guards here; in 1976 another million people crowded the square to pay him their last respects. It is also a poignant reminder of China's democracy movement, which was violently crushed in the square in 1989. }

SURROUNDING AND STUDDING the square are monuments from both the past and present, including Tiananmen, The Gate of Heavenly Peace. This podium of the powerful is the symbolic and political epicentre of China. Built in the 15th century, imperial royalty and communist leaders alike have stood atop it to view troops and proclaim the law of the land. It was from Tiananmen that Mao declared the founding of the People's Republic on 1 October 1949.

DURING THE FLAG-RAISING
ceremony, performed in Tiananmen
Square each sunrise and sunset,
soldiers march at precisely 108
paces per minute, 75 centimetres
per pace. In the build up to the 2008
Olympic Games, Beijing officials got
swept away thinking about a different
flag-raising ceremony, and proposed
to host the beach volleyball in the
square to give it a new, playful image.
The plan was dropped when they
received international feedback
that it was seen as disrespectful to
those who died here during the pro-
democracy demonstrations of 1989.

TRADITIONAL *

{ *** DESPITE BEIJING'S FAST AND FURIOUS HURTLE INTO THE FUTURE, TRADI-
TIONAL CHINA IS STILL ALIVE AND WELL IN THE CITY.** It lives down narrow
alleyways, in small tea shops, beyond temple gates and deep in the bustle of markets.
Forget the business district and mammoth sights, Beijingers' passions run highest and
their concentration is strongest on games of mah jong, time-honoured duck recipes,
market bartering and the latest family gossip. }

MANY AGE-OLD activities are considered more everyday than traditional: things like
ancient Chinese herbal remedies, riding in bicycle-powered rickshaws and flying kites.
Even the most modern families light incense sticks at the city's temples, and tea is
an unshakable addiction even after 2000 years, slurped morning, noon and night.
Beijing's parks host the practitioners of centuries-old tai chi and an individual's ability
at calligraphy is still scrutinised with a careful eye.

ONE OF THE MOST visible displays of tradition takes place at the dining table. Revered cuisines and banquets of countless dishes remain unchanged from centuries gone by, and rice has been a staple for thousands of years. Bags of chicken feet are heartily gobbled up, one-hundred-year-old eggs are sold in the markets and even many seemingly modern snacks have historic ties, such as ice-cream – first served in China around 2000 BC.

SUPERSTITIONS, like breaking uncooked noodles bringing bad luck, are widely held. The opening ceremony for Beijing's Olympics, for example, is slated for 8pm on 8 August 2008. The number 8 is associated with prosperity, so surely such a spread of eights will back up China's bid for gold medals! Social do's and don'ts like never filling your own teacup in the company of others are also still followed earnestly, and interactions are laced with traditions of propriety such as guang-xi – well-established rules for asking and giving favours.

TRADITIONAL VALUES and beliefs continue to provide the roots from which the modern city flourishes. Notions of respect, saving face and responsibility are woven tightly throughout society. While the idea of family has changed drastically in recent decades with the one-child policy and single family dwellings, extended family is still seen as a vital support system. Child-minding grandparents are a very common sight and adults work to support their ageing parents. With the end of the all-encompassing welfare system, however, many young Beijingers are putting off marriage and families until they have a healthy bank balance.

A MORE SUBTLE tradition that remains prevalent among Beijingers is the use of expressions passed down from one generation to the next. While the city has seen countless changes, modernisations and upheavals over the years, many would say that it's merely 'a new bottle filled with old wine'. Tradition lives on.

TENDER LOVING CARE*

{ * **HERBAL AND HOLISTIC REMEDIES HAVE BEEN USED IN CHINA FOR MANY CENTURIES;** one pharmacy in Beijing has been in operation since 1669. Tried and tested by millions of Chinese patients for thousands of years, Traditional Chinese Medicine (TCM) works to rebalance your body's energy and rid it of any ailments along the way. }

TREATMENTS CAN BE weird and wonderful – snake-bile syrups to expel pesky coughs, acupuncture with hundreds of needles to restore your liver. Perhaps it's just as well then that TCM aims to keep you healthy so you don't need treatment; massage, dietary changes and an ancient exercise called qi gong are commonly prescribed.

A TCM EXAMINATION COULD involve having a doctor identify your pulse (apparently there are 30 different types) or letting granny look at your tongue and whip you up a strong herbal tea. Treatment seems to work best for long-term conditions such as asthma and chronic backache.

34.

GREEN OR BLACK *

{ * **VISITING A TEAHOUSE IN BEIJING ISN'T JUST ABOUT ENJOYING A NICE CUPPA. IT'S AN ENTIRE EXPERIENCE.** Used largely for business meetings and as a more traditional alternative to the growing bar scene, teahouses are often classy affairs. It's not unusual to find a small stream bubbling through the rooms or to be serenaded by musicians playing ancient Chinese instruments similar to the viola and the flute. Small dishes of sweets and dried seeds quickly find their way to the low tables, each one often surrounded by rice paper walls for privacy. }

SIMPLY ORDERING 'tea' will result in blank stares. The dizzying array of leaves comes in three basic categories: fermented (black), non-fermented (green) and somewhere in between (Wulong). You can order tea scented with fragrant buds like jasmine or rose; tea collected from mountains or valleys; tea that tastes smoked or has virtually no flavour; tea priced as you'd expect and tea worth a minor fortune.

ENTER
THE LABYRINTH *

{ * **SQUEEZED BETWEEN WIDE BOULEVARDS, HIGH-RISES AND SHOPPING CENTRES, THE LABYRINTH OF BEIJING'S CHARMING HUTONG** is often considered the guts of the city. The first of these humble passageways were built in the Mongol Yuan dynasty and over the centuries they've multiplied to number over 6000, with names of mysterious derivation such as Dragon Whiskers Ditch Alley or Dry Flour Alley. Of varying shapes and sizes (some are just 50 centimetres wide), but generally aligned to satisfy feng shui requirements, the hutong form the city's oldest neighbourhoods and are lined with four-sided courtyard homes, simple shops, dumpling stalls and bicycle menders. On summer evenings, families escape the heat of their homes and take to the hutong, getting lost in the maze of old Beijing. }

SADLY, WRECKING BALLS are bringing the end to many of these ancient neighbourhoods, as new buildings clamour to scrape the skyline – the keen interest taken by tourists seems to be all that stands between them and oblivion.

CLICK. CLACK. The sound of small mah jong game pieces hitting the board is a common soundtrack in Beijing's parks, along its lakesides and down its alleyways. Extremely popular with the city's older crowd, weathered players can be found crowded around small tables in a state of total concentration – punctuated by whoops of joy or consternation when a point is scored. There are many different types of mah jong, but most use suits of either 13 or 16 tiles. The annual Beijing Mah Jong Tournament uses the Chinese Official Rules, developed in 1998 when the country decided to make this previously illegal gambling game into a sport.

FEEL THE CHI*

{ }

* ON PRACTICALLY ANY GREEN SPACE AVAILABLE – BE IT A LUSH PARK OR A FOOT OF GRASS BETWEEN THE LANES OF A FREEWAY – Beijingers practise the ancient art of tai chi early each morning. Centenarians lifting their legs up past their ears are living proof that this exercise-cum-self-defence art keeps you spry.

BEIJING HAS roughly 9.7 square metres of public green space for each resident. Its mass of beautiful gardens, often with ponds and paddle boats, bamboo and lotuses, offer quiet escapes from the bustle of the city, while the flowing movements of tai chi treat the whole body to a gentle but powerful work-out.

AT THE CITY CENTRE, Jinshan Park offers a gorgeous view over the golden rooftops of the Forbidden City from a hefty hill made of the earth excavated to create the palace moat. What better place to become cool, calm and energised as your mind and body work in harmony?

43.

THE STROKE OF A PEN *

{ * **THE WEIGHT OF THE BRUSH STROKES, THE FLOW OF THE INK – THERE'S MUCH MORE TO CALLIGRAPHY THAN JUST THE WRITTEN WORD.** Traditionally China's most highly esteemed art form, calligraphy dates back to the earliest day of history, yet continues to be studied, displayed, prized and sold throughout Beijing. }

ABOUT 213 BC, an official index of more than 3000 characters codified five major styles of calligraphy, and over 2000 years later all five styles of writing are still in use. However, you certainly don't have to read Chinese to appreciate calligraphy's beauty. As abstract art, it has something of the rhythmic and harmonious flow of music, and it's comparable to painting in its ability to express emotion. Watching an artist at work, brush dancing over the paper, is fascinating.

VIBRANT*

{ * **BEIJING'S ENERGY IS ALMOST TANGIBLE. ITS RIOT OF SOUNDS, HEADY AROMAS,** }
TANTALIZING TASTES and intriguing sights never fail to captivate the senses. With a
history going back five millennia, China has cultural roots stronger than fresh ginger
and it shows.

TEMPLES, THEATRE, circus performances – you'll find colour so intense it'll knock you
off your rickshaw. Festivals are celebrated throughout the year, most often dated by the
traditional Moon Calendar, and turn streets and parks into vibrant playgrounds. Even the
mundane-sounding holidays see the city splashed with bright colours and parades.

THE CITY'S MOST celebrated forms of entertainment are unique and energetic. Beijing
opera has been a sensation with audiences for the past 900 years and remains China's
most famous form of theatre – performed both in old halls in front of sunflower-spitting
grannies and to top politicians in Beijing's finest theatres. Beijingers take to the stage
with panache; performers seem to have tradition whispering guidance in one ear and a
gung-ho spirit yelling at full volume in the other.

47.

TRADITIONAL MUSICAL concerts are on the boom in Beijing. Instruments like the erhu (two-stringed fiddle) and guzheng (zither) were designed during the Shang dynasty (1700–1100 BC) and many of the folk songs have been belted out for even longer. At the other end of the spectrum, Beijing is China's rock-music mecca, with punk and DJ culture arriving in a big way.

MARTIAL ARTS have been exported around the globe and are practised in Beijing's parks, gyms and on stage. Tai chi is slow and fluid and mirrors everyday actions such as gathering water. Quick-paced kung fu is about self-defence, and stars in Hong Kong films. Qi gong is aimed at energy management; masters have been known to project their strength in miraculous ways – from healing others to driving nails through boards with their bare fingers.

A SCATTERING of China's 56 minority groups call Beijing home; adding further layers to the city's character and vibrancy. Those in traditional dress stand out against the ultra-modern cityscape. Others start up restaurants or shops, bringing the capital the flavours and goods of China's hinterlands.

COMMUNISM AND MODERNITY may have brought a good deal of grey concrete and minimalism to Beijing, but the energy of the people continues to spark and dazzle. Singing, dancing, parading, strumming, praying, leaping – it's all done with flair in Beijing.

GRACING THE STAGE*

{ * **IN BEIJING OPERA'S EARLY DAYS, PERFORMANCES WERE PUT ON AT FESTI-VALS, MARRIAGES AND EVEN FUNERALS FOR RICH PATRONS;** all were held in the open air, forcing performers to develop piercing voices that could be heard above the crowds and to wear garishly bright costumes that could be seen in poor lighting. Both female and male characters were played by men. These days, women also grace the stage but the glass-shattering pitch and vibrant clothing and make-up have remained. }

CHARACTERS USUALLY INCLUDE a young warrior displaying his martial arts skills, a woman in silk brocade singing sweetly and the mischievous Monkey King. The colour of the make-up shows character: black face-paint denotes honesty, white means crafty, red is loyalty, blue is courageous and yellow is clever and gentle.

BEIJING OPERA IS known as one of the three main theatrical systems in the world. It's said that some of Charlie Chaplin's moves were inspired by operatic star Mei Lanfang, who first took Beijing opera to the West.

51.

THE SHOW
OF 100 TRICKS*

{ *** TODAY, BEIJING ACROBATIC TROUPES WILL BLOW AWAY EVEN THE MOST BLASÉ SPECTATOR.** Young contortionists turn themselves inside out and upside down while plate-spinners whiz an amazing number of platters through the air. Dizzying feats include 'Peacock Displaying its Feathers' where a dozen or more people balance on a single bike, and 'Pagoda of Bowls' where a performer nearly ties her torso in knots while balancing a stack of bowls on one foot and another on her head. Unusual – even a little bizarre – but most definitely mesmerising. }

A FAVOURITE CHARACTER in acrobatic performances is the playful lion, which evolved from an old folk dance. The ease with which the two acrobats inside the lion's costume roll and jump belies the difficulty of this act.

CONJURING is another traditional part of performances. Unique in form and style, it can involve things like glass bowls filled with water and live fish, a lit brazier, somersaults, large robes – and the expectation of disaster.

CHINESE CIRCUS ACTS are minus the elephants, chimpanzees and clowns you might expect. Instead, routines use unexceptional objects like hoops and chairs. It is an ancient art, called 'the show of one hundred tricks'. The first records of it date back over 2000 years to the Qin dynasty (221–206 BC), so it's likely that the circus was originally a folk art which was later 'adopted' by the Imperial houses. One of the main traditional numbers is 'pole climbing'. Over the centuries movements such as swift descent and jumping from one pole to the other have been added.

CHINESE CIRCUS ACTS are minus the elephants, chimpanzees and clowns you might expect. Instead, routines use unexceptional objects like hoops and chairs. It is an ancient art, called 'the show of one hundred tricks'. The first records of it date back over 2000 years to the Qin dynasty (221–206 BC), so it's likely that the circus was originally a folk art which was later 'adopted' by the Imperial houses. One of the main traditional numbers is 'pole climbing'. Over the centuries movements such as swift descent and jumping from one pole to the other have been added.

SPRING FESTIVAL, or Chinese New Year, celebrates the Lunar New Year. It usually occurs in late January or early to mid-February. The main thing to do during Spring Festival is get together with loved ones and eat jiaozi (Chinese dumplings). Red envelopes containing money are distributed to children and there are many 'temple fairs' where everyone braves the cold to join in the fun. Roads are blocked off and folk dancers, stage shows, mimes and performers dancing on stilts take to the streets.

FESTIVE FORTUNES *

{ *** THE CHINESE LOVE TO REPLAY THEIR FOLKLORE, AND DURING THE CHINESE NEW YEAR CELEBRATIONS NO EXPENSE IS SPARED** in designing and making costumes, many of which recall epic tales of China's earlier dynasties. The winter Lantern Festival sees colourful parades ambling through the evening streets in search of airborne spirits. In March, International Labour Day leaves the entire city blanketed in bright flowers. }

THE MID-AUTUMN Moon Festival fills park benches with lovers gazing at the moon and chowing down on sweet moon cakes. The round shape of the moon represents reunion, so this day should be spent with family. The Solar New Year is also a holiday, during which people go home to see relatives.

NATIONAL DAY on October 1 is the most important national festival. Beijing is elaborately decorated, streets are lined with flowers and flags, red lanterns hang on the gates of buildings, and performances and operas are shown at all theatres.

57.

LAMA TEMPLE*

{ * **BEIJING'S TEMPLES ARE A CACOPHONY OF COLOUR, THE MOST ENIGMATIC BEING THE LAMA TEMPLE IN THE NORTHEAST OF THE CITY.** Once home to a count-cum-emperor, it became a lamasery in 1744 and remains one of the world's most renowned Tibetan Buddhist temples. Within the brightly decorated tangle of buildings the smell of yak-butter lamps mixes with the plumes of incense smoke, while crowds of worshippers prostrate themselves. }

THE DESIGN and décor is a mosaic of styles – Mongolian, Tibetan and Han. The erotic statuary inside, featuring intertwining gods and humans, was once used to educate the emperors' sons in the more pleasurable facts of life; today they are draped in yellow cloth so as not to corrupt your gaze.

IN THE FINAL HALL onlookers have to crick their necks in order to take in the truly astounding 25-metre-high Maitreya Buddha, said to have been carved from a single block of sandalwood.

61.

THE ART
OF DEFENCE*

{ ***** **AS MUCH ABOUT SPIRITUALITY AS DEFENCE, ALL CHINA'S FORMS OF MARTIAL ARTS VIEW FIGHTING AS A LAST RESORT.** Instead, it's all about balancing and directing energy and, for those on stage, spellbinding the audience with their ability to leap high off the ground (among other things). }

PRACTISING MARTIAL ARTS develops physical and mental fitness, improves self-esteem, self-control, mental agility and mental concentration. In addition, it improves general fitness, flexibility, coordination, balance, strength and self-defence skills.

THE DISCIPLINE as a whole is known as Wushu, and is rooted in centuries of tradition. Though it's deeply intertwined with Chinese culture, forms of Wushu such as tai chi and traditional kung fu have been taken up around the globe.

BOLD*

A CREATIVE STREAK SURGES THROUGH CHINA, SURFACING THROUGHOUT ITS HISTORY. It seems ten times stronger in Beijingers – partly because of their bigger window on the rest of the world, but mainly because of their boldness and confidence.

FOR HUNDREDS OF YEARS, China has produced inventions so ingenious they've become commonplace around the world: paper, printing, gunpowder and the compass. China also came up with the world's first aircraft – the kite. More recently, ancient Chinese medical techniques such as acupuncture and massage have been recognised as valuable in much of the Western world.

THE CHINESE ARE also bold politically. They built a 5000-kilometre Great Wall outside Beijing as a defence mechanism in 214 BC; dug an 1800-kilometre Grand Canal (the world's longest) in AD 609 to unify the country; and in 1971 invited not America's president, but its national table-tennis team to Beijing as the first US delegation to set foot in China for 49 years.

THE GOVERNMENT has also introduced controversial and radical programs like the one-child policy, and continues to shock the world with projects like the Three Gorges Dam, which will flood an area the size of Singapore and wash away the homes of two million people. While the world gasps and debates, the Chinese charge ahead.

65.

WHILE DECLARING ITSELF communist, the Chinese government embraces commercialism wholeheartedly; you'll find 24-hour shopping and private banks in Beijing and a Starbucks in the Forbidden City. Western countries shake their heads in confusion, but China seems to think little of its twist on political ideology.

THIS IS A CITY of contradictions. Communism snuggles up to capitalism. Affluence mingles with acute poverty. Ancient buildings lie between contemporary high-rises; ancient art forms like fan dancing are practised a few doors down from heaving discos.

THIS CITY has many faces, and as many sides to its personality as there are dishes at a Chinese banquet. Restaurants offer chic fine-dining experiences and afterwards the city's hippest crowd bumps, grinds and wiggles on packed dance floors or sips martinis in suave surroundings. In the next street, a lively market, pungent, crowded and noisy with aggressive sales pitches, keeps the traditional bartering system going strong. Birds, flowers, paintings, clothing, noodles, fish, electronics, tea, wallets, ice-cream, chicken feet, slippers… you can find it all. And in China you can buy just about any food imaginable on a stick.

ARTISTICALLY, Beijing is thriving. The rising indie film industry has produced gritty urban flicks that challenge China's past and current place in the world, and the trend has spread to canvas, with innovative, controversial art the result. The city's zealous music scene has received attention around the world for its audacious punk and rock bands. Novelists have taken a brave look at China's past and present; while many of their books are banned in China, they remain popular with Beijingers.

SPEARHEADED by Beijing, China's path forward is as unpredictable as ever. Only one thing remains certain – the city will blaze its trail boldly and imaginatively.

THE YELLOW DRAGON*

{ *** BEIJING IS IN DANGER OF BEING SWALLOWED UP BY THE GOBI DESERT, WHICH LIES A MERE 150 KILOMETRES AWAY.** Every spring sand is whipped eastward in a choking blanket that coats everything, clogs machinery and destroys crops. Beijingers call it the Yellow Dragon and wear protective plastic bags over their heads. }

WATCHING THE WINDS blowing the sands toward the capital at a rate of 2 kilometres a year, officials have been jolted into a risky reaction. They've pledged to build the Green Wall, a 3.6-million-hectare, 5700-kilometre-long belt of trees that they hope will hold back the sand and eventually reverse the effects of overgrazing and deforestation. The government has also funded research into grass strains bred in space and farming techniques for growing rice in sand.

THE QUESTION remains whether the area is too arid to support trees. And if the trees do take root they'll soak up massive amounts of groundwater, which could worsen the problem instead of solving it.

ART IN TRANSIT *

{ * **BEIJING'S MODERN ARTISTS ARE STRETCHING THEIR PAINTBRUSHES, VIEWS AND IDEAS TO ADDRESS CONTEMPORARY ISSUES.** Their work speaks of art liberated from the constraints of enforced ideology. While the government's attitude towards artistic expression is not exactly ambivalent, the artists manage daring and progressive statements, tackling issues like poverty, urbanisation, globalisation and the environment through their fresh and invigorating work. }

ONE GALLERY, in an ancient fortification gate, has 15 resident artists whose work includes everything from sculpture to papercutting to performance art, ink and wash, printmaking, posters, lithographs, oils and photography. As artists struggle with the changing face and shifting culture of China, you may find re-imagined snapshots of history in a din of spills and drips, or a hazy white emptiness, perhaps the empty canvas of the future. Work might mix cuteness with calligraphy, or present a humorous edge – all representative of a culture in transit.

WHEN THE QUESTION arises as to what to do with a deceased leader's body, pickling doesn't immediately come to mind. But the Chinese government decided nothing short of 'preservation in perpetuity' would do for Mao, and the doctor was called upon. The body, in all of its formaldehyde glory, went on display in a mausoleum built in Tiananmen Square.

PLAYING WITH FIRE*

{ * **DISCOVERED BY CHANCE AROUND 2000 YEARS AGO BY A CHINESE CHEF, GUNPOWDER WAS INITIALLY USED TO WARD OFF EVIL SPIRITS.** This eventually turned into noisy displays of gunpowder shot skyward – now commonly known as fire-works. This isn't to say that the Chinese didn't catch on to the killing power of the powder, but even their use of it for such ends had a creative bent. They targeted their enemies with fire arrows (bamboo firecrackers attached to an arrow) and 'ground rats' (bamboo firecrackers that buzzed on the ground when lit, to the terror of horses). }

IN 1994, Beijing city planners outlawed firecrackers in hopes of lowering pollution. Twelve years later, oddly, the ban was lifted even though the city had tightened environmental laws in preparation for the Olympics. But Beijingers seem to be in full support; at Chinese New Year more than 600,000 boxes of explosives are sold from 24-hour firecracker shops.

74.

FOOD
GLORIOUS FOOD*

{ * **BEIJINGERS ALWAYS DO THINGS ON A GRAND SCALE – AND THAT INCLUDES EATING. BANQUETS ARE THE ZENITH OF CHINESE DINING,** held for festivities like weddings, to clinch business deals, or to simply impress guests in no uncertain terms. To avoid looking tight-fisted, the host orders more than the guests could possibly eat. Rice is looked upon as cheap filler and rarely appears among the ten or more courses that are served. }

THESE DAYS Beijing's restaurants cater to virtually every palate – lasagne, souvlaki, yakisoba and bagels grace the menu alongside dishes from Sichuan, Guangdong, Shandong, Shanghai and Hangzhou.

WHILE PEKING DUCK, Beijing's most famous dish, is served at most tourist-trodden restaurants, only the locals can tell you where to get the crispiest duck in town. Coated in molasses and roasted over a fruitwood fire, the boneless bird arrives at the table adorned with shallots, plum sauce and crepes.

77.

AMBITIOUS*

{ *** BEIJINGERS HAVE THEIR EYES ON THE FUTURE. APPARENTLY THEY LIKE WHAT THEY SEE, AS THEY'RE RACING FULL THROTTLE TOWARDS IT.** With an economy growing as fast as bamboo, Beijing is a giant on the global scene – a position many believe will mature into it becoming the world's economic leader. }

THAT MODERNISATION HAS collided with the city in a big way is evident in the flashy architecture and the plethora of top-of-the-line, brand-name retail goods. Beijing's wide boulevards buzz with activity; everyone has somewhere to be, mobile in one hand, designer bag in the other. Buses are crammed past capacity, thousands of bicycles crowd the streets, the subway bullets beneath the surface and taxis race through the mayhem. Increasingly sophisticated and increasingly chic, the more affluent citizens of Beijing have their eyes on a global horizon.

ALL OF THE RECENT modernisation, however, has left Beijing's environment worse for wear. Beijing is determined to have its act cleaned up by the time the Olympics arrive in 2008. Cleaner air, water and streets are all on its ambitious 'to do' list.

79.

IT'S HARDLY SURPRISING that 'gung-ho' is a phrase originating in China. Beijingers embody it to the fullest. Their energy is seemingly unstoppable and their resourcefulness unparalleled. From students to top politicians, their web of personal contacts and connections (called guang-xi) helps them get where and what they want, often through the back door.

AFTER DECADES OF blue Mao suits, Beijing designers are wielding their scissors and needles again, making a fast and furious comeback. Many of their designs take the high-necked, narrow-cut, silky qipao (the quintessential Chinese frock) as a starting point but raise the hemlines, turn up the volume on the material and make it chic enough to win approval on Western catwalks. Their designs are very hip, very modern and very Beijing.

BEIJING'S CITIZENS also seem to be always awake. Older citizens are generally early risers, exercising out of doors at the crack of dawn; much of the city's younger populace, in contrast, bar-hop until the wee hours of the morning. Many spend their free time relaxing in parks, shopping or visiting family. Department stores, shopping malls and streets lined with chain stores provide retail therapy to the designer-heeled. From Gucci to Gap, if you can think of it, it's probably for sale in Beijing.

THERE'S A DEFINITE vibe of 'survival of the fittest' in the air – something which must come as second nature in a city of nearly 15 million where starvation and violence were written on a rather recent page of history. As the restrictions of communism ease off and capitalism is embraced, Beijingers are busy perfecting the arts of shopping, designing, building, climbing the economic ladder and enjoying the view ahead.

ONE EYE ON THE BALL*

{ * **UNTIL FAIRLY RECENTLY, FOOTBALL WAS ALMOST UNKNOWN IN BEIJING.** Then the city wowed itself by qualifying for the 2002 World Cup and Beijingers went football-crazy overnight. Stadiums are now packed out, drinking holes pay homage with huge TV screens and Beijingers talk about the sport with as much gusto as their European counterparts. }

THE OLYMPIC FOOTBALL team is racing to get in shape for the 2008 Games. The new Olympic football stadium will cover a floor area of 78,000 square metres, and has a capacity of 60,000.

THE LOCAL FOOTBALL CLUB, Beijing ClubFootball, has developed rapidly and offers five-, seven- and eleven-a-side leagues with several divisions. Coaching is available, encouraging young people to get involved. Keep your eye on the ball…

82.

BEIJING RISING*

{ * **AMID THE SPLENDOUR OF ITS ANCIENT GATES AND PALACES, BEIJING SEEMS TO SPROUT NEW HIGH-RISES ON A DAILY BASIS.** Skyscrapers range from posh and classy to tacky pinnacles – new designs, unlike anything seen before in China, scream that Beijing is innovative. The headquarters for the state television network is a brightly coloured continuous loop 230 metres high, like a moving letter 'Z'. Its companion structure looks like a trapezoidal boot. }

AS OLD NEIGHBOURHOODS are bulldozed to make room for these modern creations, Beijingers wait with bated breath to see what form they'll take. Even the antiquated Great Wall has been given a new lease of life which would render it unrecognisable to the thousands of labourers that raised it in 204 BC – it's being used as one of the world's most unusual party venues. Annual 24-hour 'Illuminate the Great Wall' festivals draw hundreds of party-goers from Beijing, as well as top DJs, live musicians and art installations.

85.

THE OLYMPIC
SPIRIT*

{ * **THE OLYMPICS ARE ON THE SLOW BOAT TO CHINA AND BEIJING FEELS LIKE** }
IT'S FINALLY GETTING THE RECOGNITION IT DESERVES. Meanwhile, the rest of
the world murmurs about whether China's human rights record should disqualify it
from playing host or whether the Games really are above politics.

BEIJINGERS SEEM to be taking little notice. They're too busy painting the logo on anything that will stand still, pumping out T-shirts, landscaping new parks, priming their
teams and building 37 new gymnasiums and stadiums and nine new training centres.

A DISTINCTLY POSITIVE result is that the Olympics come with a prerequisite: Beijing
has to do an environmental clean-up before the opening ceremony in 2008. Promises
made by the city include having 90% of public buses and 60% of taxis running on
natural gas; ousting 110 polluting factories to the city's outskirts; and lowering air-
pollution levels to those presently found in Paris.

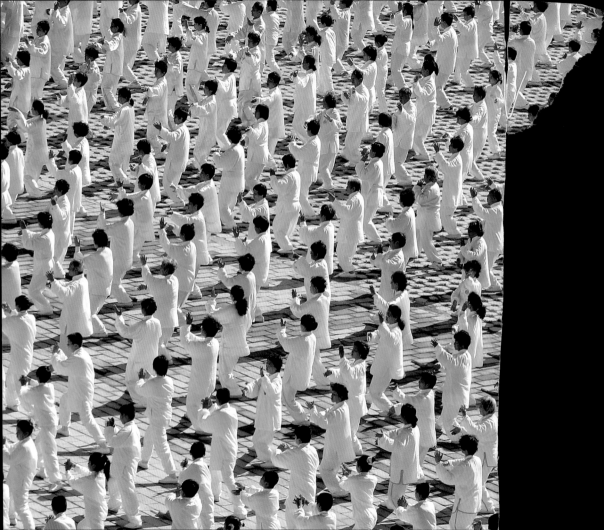

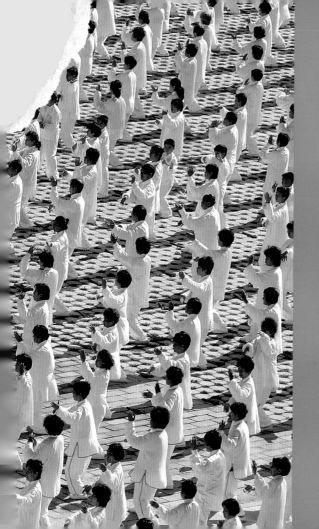

IN PREPARATION FOR THE 2008
Olympics, Beijing has embarked
on a major building frenzy that
encompasses not only stadiums
and high-rises but also more
unusual structures. One man has
constructed an enormous kite called
the 'Olympic Swallow' dedicated to
the Games, with a dream of having
it flown in the Olympic skies. Made
of 60 three-metre lengths of
bamboo, 100 metres of fabric
and 4 kilograms of glue, the kite is
3 kilometres long. The diligent
engineer spent five years creating it.

90.

GOLD STAR

REALLY, BEIJING SHOULD GET A HANDFUL OF GOLD STARS FOR ITS MASSIVE SIGHTS, HUGE CHARACTER AND FOR KEEPING A SURPRISE HIDDEN AROUND EACH BEND. BUT WITH JUST ONE TO BESTOW, WE'RE GOING TO GO GREEN AND AWARD IT FOR HAVING THE LARGEST FLEET OF NATURAL-GAS BUSES IN THE WORLD – A TOTAL OF 1630, AND MORE ON THE WAY.

MY PERFECT DAY

KORINA MILLER

{ * Beijing is often best early in the morning, when a calm blankets the city, and mornings in Beijing are best spent in a park watching the older community absorbed in the ancient exercises of tai chi or qi gong, with their toes up round their noses. After all that serenity, the bedlam of a market is in order; if it's the weekend, Panjiayuan (or the Dirt Market) is tops for arts, antiques and mingling with folks from the surrounding countryside. After that, recover over a bottomless cup of tea at one of the oh-so-modern and intensely comfortable teahouses. Hop on a bike and get lost in Beijing's hutong for a while, taking a peek at the city's past. If time is on your side, take in one of Beijing's gob-smacking sights – either Red Gate Gallery for modern art or the Lama

Temple with its other-worldly atmosphere. Then scale the hill in Jinshan Park to watch the sun sink over the golden rooftops of the Forbidden City. Slide back down the hill to the nearby lakesides for an outdoor apéritif, then on to dinner – the choice of cuisine in Beijing is positively endless.

}

KORINA LIVED THE FIRST 18 YEARS OF HER LIFE ON VANCOUVER ISLAND. Since then she hasn't stayed in any one place for very long, taking in parts of Asia, India, Egypt, Europe, the South Pacific and South and Central America. Along the way she picked up a degree in Communications and an MA in Migration Studies. Her first venture into China was in 1997 when she landed a job researching cooperatives and ecotourism in Shanghai and Lijiang. Her subsequent travels through China have taken her from the Manchurian border in the north to the Tibetan Plateau in the southwest. Since researching Lonely Planet's *Best of Beijing*, she hasn't stopped raving about the country's heady capital.

PHOTO CREDITS

{

PAGE 2 The Beijing sun glows through a man's umbrella
Anthony Cassidy/Getty Images

PAGE 4 A man rides a tricycle through heavy fog on the outskirts of Beijing
Cancan Chu/Getty Images

PAGE 6 Watching the world go by Beijing style
Yann Layma/Getty Images

PAGE 8 Chinese tourists rest for a moment after touring the Forbidden City
Ray Laskowitz/Lonely Planet Images

PAGE 10 Carved dogs atop each pillar of the bridge across Kunming Lake at the Summer Palace
Ian Cumming/Axiom

PAGE 12 Men play checkers at Tiantan Park
Glenn Beanland/Lonely Planet Images

PAGE 15 A young local girl enjoys dressing up
Krzysztof Dydynski/Lonely Planet Images

PAGE 16 Detail of the decorative main archway that forms the entrance to Yonghe Gong (Lama Temple)
Damien Simonis/Lonely Planet Images

PAGE 19 Workmen on scaffolding beside a giant poster of Chairman Mao
Mark Henley/Impact Photos

PAGE 20 An elderly man stands in one of the courtyards of the Forbidden City
Phil Weymouth/Lonely Planet Images

PAGES 22–3 The 17-arch bridge over Kunming Lake at the Summer Palace
Luca da Ros/4Corners Images

PAGE 25 A winter view of part of the Great Wall of China and surrounding hills
Peter Solness/Lonely Planet Images

PAGE 26 A socialist-realist monument at Chairman Mao Zedong's mausoleum, Tiananmen Square
Krzysztof Dydynski/Lonely Planet Images

PAGES 28–9 Cyclists pass Tiananmen Gate as the sun sets over Tiananmen Square
David Noton/Getty Images

PAGE 30 Walking past 1960s-era propaganda on the wall of a hutong
Natalie Behring/Panos Pictures

PAGE 33 Brushes for sale in Zuanwu in the Qianmen district
Phil Weymouth/Lonely Planet Images

PAGE 35 Traditional Chinese medicine on display at Tongrentang, the oldest shop in the Qianmen district
Lionel Derimais/APL/Corbis

PAGE 36 China One Tea House and Bar at Houhai Lake
Greg Elms/Lonely Planet Images

PAGE 38 Riding a bicycle-cart along Xiaojiao Hutong in Dong-cheng district
Phil Weymouth/Lonely Planet Images

PAGES 40–1 Mah jong tiles
Keren Su/Lonely Planet Images

PAGE 42 A tai chi master practises his art in Beijing
Keren Su/Getty Images

PAGE 44 A man paints Chinese characters in water with a long modified brush
Justin Guariglia/APL/Corbis

CITIESCAPE
BEIJING

OCTOBER 2006

**PUBLISHED BY LONELY PLANET
PUBLICATIONS PTY LTD**
ABN 36 005 607 983
90 Maribyrnong St, Footscray,
Victoria 3011, Australia
www.lonelyplanet.com

Printed through Colorcraft Ltd, Hong Kong.
Printed in China.

PHOTOGRAPHS
Many of the images in this book are available
for licensing from Lonely Planet Images.
www.lonelyplanetimages.com

ISBN 1 74104 934 2

© Lonely Planet 2006
© photographers as indicated 2006

LONELY PLANET OFFICES
AUSTRALIA Locked Bag 1, Footscray, Victoria 3011
Telephone 03 8379 8000 Fax 03 8379 8111
Email talk2us@lonelyplanet.com.au

USA 150 Linden St, Oakland, CA 94607
Telephone 510 893 8555 TOLL FREE 800 275 8555
Fax 510 893 8572 Email info@lonelyplanet.com

UK 72–82 Rosebery Ave, London EC1R 4RW
Telephone 020 7841 9000 Fax 020 7841 9001
Email go@lonelyplanet.co.uk

Publisher ROZ HOPKINS
Commissioning Editor ELLIE COBB
Editors JOCELYN HAREWOOD, VANESSA BATTERSBY
Design MARK ADAMS
Layout Designer INDRA KILFOYLE
Image Researcher PEPI BLUCK
Pre-press Production GERARD WALKER
Project Managers ANNELIES MERTENS, ADAM MCCROW
Publishing Planning Manager JO VRACA
Print Production Manager GRAHAM IMESON